DOGS SET I

POODLES

Heidi Mathea
ABDO Publishing Company

visit us at
www.abdopublishing.com

Printed in the United States of America, North Mankato, Minnesota.
042010
092010

 PRINTED ON RECYCLED PAPER

Cover Photo: Corbis
Interior Photos: Animals Animals p. 17; Getty Images pp. 4–5, 11, 13, 18;
     iStockphoto pp. 19, 20, 21; Peter Arnold pp. 6–7, 9, 15

Editor: Megan M. Gunderson
Art Direction & Cover Design: Neil Klinepier

Library of Congress Cataloging-in-Publication Data

Mathea, Heidi, 1979-
  Poodles / Heidi Mathea.
       p. cm. -- (Dogs)
  Includes index.
  ISBN 978-1-61613-409-9
  1. Poodles--Juvenile literature. I. Title.
  SF429.P85M29 2011
  636.72'8--dc22
                                          2010013419

CONTENTS

The Dog Family 4

Poodles 6

What They're Like 8

Coat and Color 10

Size 12

Care 14

Feeding 16

Things They Need 18

Puppies 20

Glossary 22

Web Sites 23

Index 24

THE DOG FAMILY

All dogs are related to the gray wolf. So, how did they become man's best friend? The history of dogs and humans is long and rich.

Historians believe wolves began hanging around campsites hoping to find food. Humans soon realized these animals would make great hunting partners.

As lifestyles changed, humans **bred** new dogs to fit their needs. Dogs began herding, guarding, and keeping people company. Today, more than 400 dog breeds exist.

They all belong to the family **Canidae**.

One of the oldest dog **breeds** is the poodle. Poodles are known for their **unique** haircuts. But, there is much more to these special dogs. Poodles are smart, affectionate animals.

Like the first dogs, poodles started as hunting partners.

POODLES

What do you think of when you hear the word *poodles*? Many people imagine dogs with poofy hair tied in bows. But, this **breed** is not dainty!

The poodle breed began in Germany. The first poodles were water dogs. Hunters used them to **retrieve** ducks and geese from water during a hunt.

Poodles have thick coats that become very heavy when wet. To help the dogs swim better, hunters began shaving their coats. The hunters left patches of fur to protect sensitive areas from cold water. This is how the well-known poodle clip started.

These hunting dogs soon became known as great family pets. Their popularity spread worldwide. The **American Kennel Club** recognized the poodle in 1887. Today, the poodle is one of the top ten most popular dog **breeds** in the United States.

The word poodle is taken from a German word meaning "to splash in the water."

WHAT THEY'RE LIKE

Poodles come in three sizes. That means there is a size to fit most owners! From smallest to largest there are toy, miniature, and standard poodles.

The poodle's happy nature helped make the **breed** popular. This graceful dog is also very intelligent. It can easily learn new tricks and commands.

Poodles make great family pets. They want to be involved in every activity! Miniature and standard poodles in particular are good with children. These affectionate poodles will watch over young people and are always ready to play.

The poodle loves to be the center of attention!

COAT AND COLOR

Poodles have thick, curly coats. Adult show poodles must display an English saddle, continental, or sporting clip. For all three clips, a poodle's face, throat, feet, and tail base are shaved. And, the tail ends in a fluffy ball called a pompon.

For the English saddle clip, the front legs are shaved, leaving puffs of hair. Each back leg has two shaved bands. A short blanket of hair is left on the hindquarters. A curved area is shaved out of each **flank**.

For the continental clip, all four legs are shaved. Puffs of hair are left on the front legs. Bracelets appear on the back legs. The hindquarters are shaved, but pompons may be left on the hips.

For the sporting clip, the hair is trimmed to one inch (3 cm) in length. This can be done with clippers or scissors. A cap is left on the head.

Poodles come in a variety of solid colors. Most show poodles are either black or white. But they may also be blue, brown, silver, apricot, or cream.

If a poodle's hair is allowed to grow long, it will form ropelike cords. Then, it is called a corded poodle.

SIZE

The three poodle sizes are based on height. This measurement is taken from the ground to the dog's shoulders.

The toy poodle is the smallest at 10 inches (25 cm) or fewer. A miniature poodle stands more than 10 inches but fewer than 15 inches (38 cm). The standard poodle is the tallest. It is more than 15 inches tall.

Because poodle size is based on height, weight varies within the **breed**. Poodles range from just 7 pounds (3 kg) up to 55 pounds (25 kg)!

A well-bred poodle has a noble face with flat cheekbones. Its head is round, and its **muzzle** is long and straight. The oval eyes are set wide apart. They give the poodle an alert, smart look. This active dog's tail is high-set, straight, and **docked**.

**Big or small,
poodles are lovable!**

CARE

Poodles have been serving as pets for hundreds of years. For many people, there is no better **breed**. Poodles are gentle, loving, playful, and carefree. They can live in any size home. But they are active and require daily exercise. Poodles must also receive lots of love and attention!

One bonus for many owners is that the poodle's coat doesn't **shed**. But it does require a lot of work. Poodles need regular brushing and professional grooming. Brushing alone can take a couple of hours each week. And grooming can get expensive.

To remain healthy, a poodle must visit a veterinarian at least twice a year. The veterinarian can **spay** or **neuter** puppies. He or she will also provide **vaccines**.

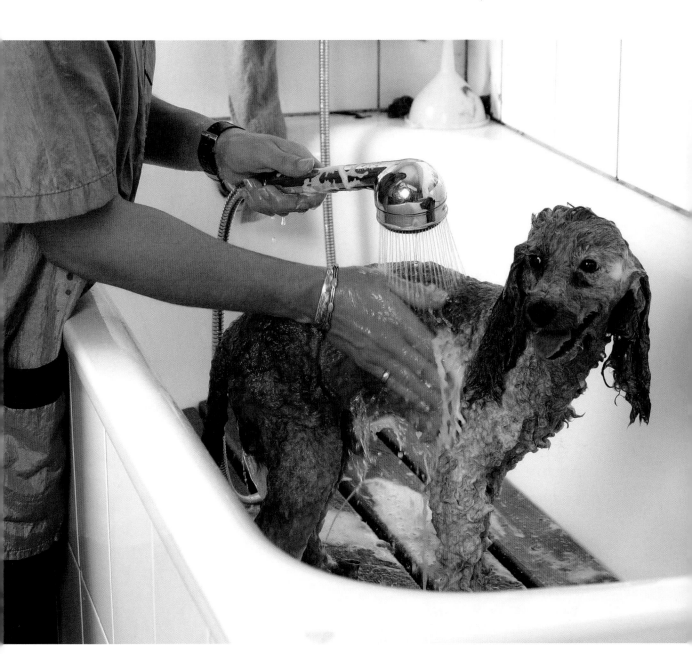

When bathing your poodle, be sure to protect its eyes and ears.

FEEDING

Proper **nutrition** will help keep your poodle's beautiful coat in good shape. A high-quality commercial food will provide a well-balanced diet. Your veterinarian can help you choose the best food for your dog.

When you buy a puppy, find out what it has been eating. Continue that diet to avoid upsetting your pet. A small puppy needs several meals a day. By six months, it will need to eat only twice daily.

Your poodle may act like it wants human food. But don't be fooled! Avoid feeding the dog table scraps. And be careful not to overfeed it. Lots of food and doggie treats could make your pet overweight!

Water is important to an active **breed** such as the poodle. Keep a full dish of water next to the dog's food bowl. Be sure to change it daily.

A well-fed poodle
makes a happy pet.

THINGS THEY NEED

Poodles are **bred** to be around people. They crave love and attention. To be at their happiest, poodles need to be where their families are. So they should live indoors. Still, poodles sometimes like to go somewhere quiet. Provide your pet with a soft dog bed or a crate for resting.

Exercise is important to this breed. However, a poodle will enjoy walking or running only

Exercise is a great way to bond with your pet.

18

Sometimes, even a poodle needs to rest.

with its owner. These activities will keep you and
your pet in good shape!

Purchase a leash, a collar, and an identification
tag for your poodle. An identification tag includes
your name and contact information. Should your pet
become lost, this will help it get returned to you.

PUPPIES

After mating, a female poodle is **pregnant** for about nine weeks. She gives birth to tiny, helpless puppies. The puppies cannot see or hear for about two weeks. They need their mother to care for and feed them.

If you think a poodle is right for you, find a reliable **breeder**. He or she can provide cuddly puppies. Poodle rescue organizations may also have poodles that need good homes.

Training is an important job for any dog owner. You must begin training your puppy the same day you bring it home. Over time, introduce your pet to new people and places. This will help make it even more gentle. With lots of tender loving care, a poodle will make a great pet for as many as 15 years!

Poodle puppies love to cuddle with their owners!

21

GLOSSARY

American Kennel Club - an organization that studies and promotes interest in purebred dogs.

breed - a group of animals sharing the same ancestors and appearance. A breeder is a person who raises animals. Raising animals is often called breeding them.

Canidae (KAN-uh-dee) - the scientific Latin name for the dog family. Members of this family are called canids. They include domestic dogs, wolves, jackals, foxes, and coyotes.

docked - cut short.

flank - the side of an animal or a person between the ribs and the hip.

muzzle - an animal's nose and jaws.

neuter (NOO-tuhr) - to remove a male animal's reproductive organs.

nutrition - that which provides energy and promotes growth, maintenance, and repair.

pregnant - having one or more babies growing within the body.

retrieve - to locate and bring in.

shed - to cast off hair, feathers, skin, or other coverings or parts by a natural process.

spay - to remove a female animal's reproductive organs.

unique - being the only one of its kind.

vaccine (vak-SEEN) - a shot given to prevent illness or disease.

WEB SITES

To learn more about poodles, visit ABDO Publishing Company on the World Wide Web at **www.abdopublishing.com**. Web sites about poodles are featured on our Book Links page. These links are routinely monitored and updated to provide the most current information available.

INDEX

A
American Kennel
    Club 7

B
bed 18
body 10, 12
breeder 20

C
Canidae (family) 5
character 5, 7, 8,
    12, 14, 16, 18,
    21
clips 5, 7, 10, 11
coat 5, 6, 7, 10, 11,
    14, 16
collar 19
color 11
crate 18

E
exercise 14, 18, 19
eyes 12

F
feet 10
food 16, 20

G
Germany 6
grooming 14

H
head 10, 11, 12
health 14, 16, 19
history 4, 5, 6, 7,
    14
hunting 6, 7

L
leash 19
legs 10
life span 21

M
muzzle 12

N
neuter 14

P
puppies 14, 16, 20,
    21

R
reproduction 20

S
senses 20
shoulders 12
size 8, 12, 16, 20
spay 14

T
tail 10, 12
training 21

U
United States 7

V
vaccines 14
veterinarian 14, 16

W
water 16